THE DEARNE VALLEY RAILWAY

C. T. Goode

1986

ISBN 0/9508239/9/6

72 Woodland Drive, Anlaby, Hull. HU10 7HX.

Introduction

This is the history of a somewhat different but down-to-earth promotion of the Lancashire & Yorkshire Company, laid down for the express purpose of moving large quantities of coal without fuss or spectacle, which it managed to do successfully for the whole of its life. Romance was there, however, for the finely-tuned railway buff, in the way in which such an interloper could come all the way from distant Wakefield and plant its foreign habits adjacent to the incumbert Great Northern Railway at Doncaster. The signals were unusual and were serviced from Wakefield. The engines were the wrong shape and there was that rare looking tank engine with its jaunty maroon coach and retractable steps. Nobody seems to have taken a photograph of it crossing the Conisbrough Viaduct; indeed, nobody seems to have taken many shots of movement on the line at all, so that those included in this little book are rare indeed.

Nevertheless I hope the reading will prove interesting and evoke some of the atmosphere of a useful railway. I am indebted to the Public Record Office Kew and the House of Lords Record Office Westminster, as well as Leeds City Library, the West Yorks. County Archive and the National Railway Museum for much documentation. A mention here also to J. Bennett, L. Franks and Trevor Sutcliffe for interesting items which appear herein.

C. Tony Goode.

Anlaby, Hull.

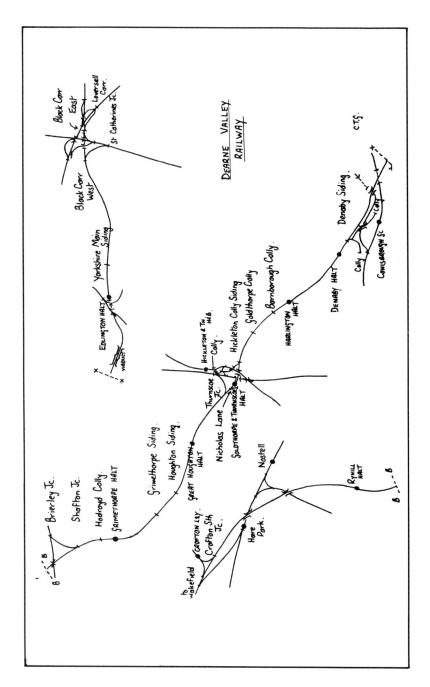

DEARNE VALLEY RAILWAY

The Dearne Valley Railway

It never fails to surprise one how the railway system in this country managed to develop, and how lines put down in what appears to have been a haphazard way seem in the end to have had, in most cases, a real purpose. At the end of the nineteenth century the South Yorkshire coalfield was beginning to make its presence felt with an output of good quality steam coal from a field which stretched from Barnsley to the Trent, and several collieries were planned for the early years of the twentieth century in this fruitful area. Railways were, of course, already in position, with the Hull & Barnsley running in from the north east almost into Barnsley itself, the Swinton & Knottingley Joint line of the Midland and North Eastern Railways passing north-south and the old hand at the game, the Great Central running east-west along the southern edge of the coalfield. Along the northern edge ran the Lancashire & Yorkshire company, a plain, influential no-nonsense sort of concern whose main route ran through Wakefield towards Goole.

Having the coal on the other side of its boundary fence, and realising the rewards to be gained from transporting it either for local use or for export via the Humber, the L & Y was naturally interested in any new railway proposition which might tap new collieries in the South Yorkshire coalfield whose names, Grimethorpe, Houghton, Hickleton, Denaby and Cadeby, would soon become famous. Such a new line would give access to the markets of the West Riding and Lancashire on the one hand, and the farmlands of the Eastern Counties and London on the other by means of links with existing railways over which the ports of Goole and Hull might also be reached.

The L & Y was, from the outset, most interested in the project, with Sir George Armytage, its Chairman as well as Chairman of the major company. Mr. H. Marriott was also joint traffic superintendent. The new company was known as the Dearne Valley Railway, nominally an independent company and not incorporated with the L & Y or with anyone else. Directors were colliery owners in the area in question and the line was sponsored by Hickleton, Houghton and Carlton Main Collieries, whence came Messrs. J. J. Addy, C. E. Hunter, R. Armitage and E. Hague. Robert Armitage was a director of Hickleton Main and other companies. Carlton Main was originally the property of the Yorks. & Derbyshire Coal & Iron Company and was a partner with Grimethorpe. It was one of the older collieries and dated from 1876. Grimethorpe came in 1896 and was sunk on the estates of Mr. F. J. S. Foljambe. The first coal had left Manvers Main in 1870, Houghton in 1878 and Hickleton Main in 1894.

The first suggestion for a new railway came from Mr. J. W. H. White of the engineering firm of Mammatt & White of Leeds, with the proposal to the L & Y Board that a suitable railway be provided from the Horbury direction, on the L & Y main line west of Wakefield. No action on this was taken by the L & Y; however, the Dearne Valley Railway Act was incorporated in 1897 to run from the H & B line near Hemsworth to the GN and GE Joint line at Black Carr, south east of Doncaster. The link with the H & B is interesting, for that particular company was small, independent and forceful and well placed to take coal for export. From 1898 a five year working agreement was signed, with mutual running powers. This did not please the promoters of the DVR Bill who had held their first meeting at the Royal Station Hotel in Sheffield on 8th

January, 1897 under the chairmanship of Ernest Hague. All along there had been a covert wish to link the DVR with the L & Y in some shape or form, and Mr. Addy had written to Mr. Aspinall, the General Manager of the L & Y to persuade his company to run from Barnsley to Grimethorpe Colliery over the GC Houghton Main branch (presumably with GC permission!). The two men met in Manchester in August 1899. Committee meeting notes of the times make little mention of any action by either side. As well as the H & B, both the GN and GE had adopted powers to work the line when completed, but nothing transpired in this event.

According to the terms of the original Act, five years were allowed to complete the railway and seven years for the dock, wharf and lay-bye which were scheduled for construction near Denaby, the last two on the north bank of the river Don at Mexborough. In the case of the former the Dearne was to be widened and deepened on both sides. By an Act of 30th July 1900 the completion times were extended to 6th August 1905 for the railway and 6th August 1908 for the river works.

A letter from Mr. Addy to Mr. Aspinall of 1st August 189 asked for an L & Y connection with the DVR, either over the GC or over a new line from a junction in the parish of Felkirk to the vicinity of Horbury. Addy asked for a guarantee of traffic and for a positive statement as to how such traffic would be worked. The reply was evasive and there was not progress until the summer of 1900 when it was suggested that the L & Y might wish to purchase the new line and finish the south eastern end of it themselves. Aspinall was again evasive, but it was clear that he neither wished to purchase nor to start work on the connecting line. Most likely his Board were piqued over the interest shown by the H & B over the arrangements. No other company should be involved in any scheme until the L & Y had been given first refusal. The H & B had obtained running powers to Grimethorpe and Houghton Main, in exchange

Brierley Jc. looking towards Hull. DVR off right.   *C. T. Goode*

for DVR powers to Monckton Main and Carlton Main in the Cudworth area, in H & B territory. Addy and Hague, according to a report on the meeting of 17th July, 1900, were still anxious for the L & Y to purchase the DVR, provided that the former would complete the line to Black Carr. 'If we dispose of the line, we wish it to be worked by a good company, and prefer the L & Y'. Smooth words indeed.

At a Board meeting on 25th October, 1900 the DVR directors had the company of a referee in the person of Mr. H. Lambert, a former GWR Manager. Here it was decided that a link with the L & Y would be made, to be constructed either by the L & Y or jointly with them and the DVR. The DVR would undertake to complete the Black Carr end in three years from 31st December, 1900 if the L & Y would build the line north to Crofton. This was ratified on 29th October, 1900 and both lines would be built at the same time and contracts would expire on the same date. By the DVR Junction Act of 26th July, 1901 the new line would be constructed in three years from the end of August, together with running powers awarded to the L & Y from one month previously, no doubt for the movement of materials off the nearly completed works. The branch to Denaby Colliery was to be finished by the same date. A single line was to be laid at first, but sufficient land was acquired for a double track. Connections were to be made with the S & K Joint line in the Goldthorpe area which afforded another outlet to Goole and Hull and other important places. The Dearne Valley Junction Railway was to be of 5 miles 63 chains running from the Wakefield-Goole line at Crofton, 210 yd. east of the West Riding & Grimsby line from Hare Park, generally south east to the DVR proper at Shafton. There was also to be a spur at Crofton turning towards Goole. The capital involved was £246,000, and the L & Y released a further £200,000 to the DVR in return for which they would work the line. In effect, therefore, they became one third of the owning force of the DVR and fielded two directors, Sir George Armytage and E. B. Fielden. At an initial Board meeting on 14th October, 1902 at the Queen's Hotel in Leeds Sir George was the Chairman and it was decided that subsequent meetings would move to the L & Y Headquarters at Hunts Bank, Manchester, once the Crofton branch was completed. Another L & Y man, Mr. Sebastian Meyer, would continue as the DVR General Manager at a salary of £300 per annum until the Crofton branch was ready, but would then suffer a reduction as its Secretary to £150 per annum.

Construction of the Junction line was let to Whittaker Bros for £145,760. On the death of the Engineer, Mr. J. W. H. White, Mr. S. R. Kay succeeded. The L & Y appointed its Chief Engineer as consultant engineer of the DVR at £100 per annum. Mr. Clayton was Maintenance Engineer at £20 yearly as from 1st January 1903, though after possible complaint this was increased to £50. Grimethorpe and Houghton Collieries were linked to Brierley Junction on the H & B as from 19th March, 1902, traffic probably operated by contractor's or colliery engines. The H & B had offered to work the coal with their engines, but it was eventually decided that traffic should be exchanged at Brierley instead, certainly after 1905. The NER had hackles raised over the movement of coal to Hull which had gone via Brierley Jc., Hensall and Goole. There was some correspondence between Aspinall and George Gibb of the NER on this subject between 1903-5 in which it was pointed out that the NER had not been consulted about through rates. The upshot was that coal was now to be encouraged to pass to the ports via Thurnscoe Jc. and the S & K as convenient. No fixed ideas were laid down and the traffic was to be left 'to flow as it may be consigned'.

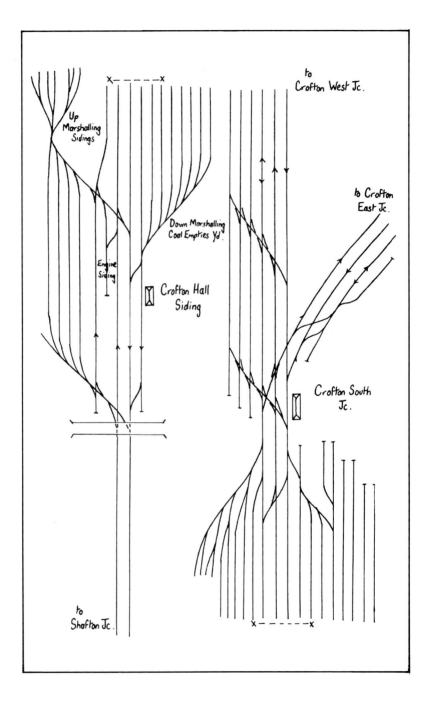

to
Crofton West Jc.

Up
Marshalling
Sidings

to Crofton
East Jc.

Down Marshalling
Coal Empties Yd.

Engine
Siding

Crofton Hall
Siding

Crofton South
Jc.

to
Shafton Jc.

The Dearne Valley Junction Railway opened on 6th March, 1905, and 7/6- per hour was paid to the L & Y for the use of Class A engines and guards working over the railway. By May 1906 more powerful engines were attracting 10/- an hour, though this did include the services of guards and brake vans. An L & Y engine was provided to work exclusively on the DVR at £15 per week, which included the crew and a cleaner. The company were to find coal, water, shunter and a shed. The latter was probably that at Black Carr which was opened in 1908.

Completion dates for the sections of Dearne Valley track are as follows:

Shafton to Grimethorpe and Houghton 19th March, 1902.
Houghton to Thurnscoe 13th March, 1905.
Thurnscoe to Hickleton 26th February, 1906.
Hickleton to Denaby 12th March, 1906.
Denaby to Cadeby 6th August, 1904.
and the scenic section to Black Carr West 7th October, 1908.

Mr. Worthington was appointed Consultant Engineer from 1st January, 1903 to 29th May, 1905 at £100 per annum, and after this time he went to the Midland Railway staff. Mr. R. H. Clayton, the Resident Engineer, received £20 yearly from 1st January, 1903, increased to £50 per annum one year later. The branch to Denaby was authorised in a separate Act of 1904 which gave the company licence to behave as it chose in respect of a bridge over the Don which could be either a high, fixed link or a lower opening one. Any alteration would be at the expense of the Navigation and, if movable, would

Bridges in the Goldthorpe area, looking east. Beyond the road bridge can be seen the dismantled H & B bridge which carried the Wath branch. C. T. Goode

be operated and serviced at the Navigation's expense, a canny manoeuvre. The contractors were Messrs. Gates & Hogg, who were authorised to work the branch traffic from completion on 12th March, 1906 until handing over to the L & Y on 4th August. The tender for the bridge over the Don was £4,979.

The DVR bridge crossing the H & B line at Cadeby, just before reaching Conisbrough Viaduct.   *C. T. Goode*

To cover the Dearne Valley Junction Railway in more detail now. Railway No.1 ran from a junction between the L & Y Goole main line and the WR & G spur from Hare Park, running south east to Shay Lane. The general gradient was a rise at 1 in 92 to 1 in 120. Railway No.2 was the curve from Shay Lane running round to the north east to the overbridge just west of Crofton station, of 2 furlongs radius.

Shay Lane crossed the new line by a 35ft. span 15ft. high, while further on the WR & G line was crossed by a skew 26ft. span at 14ft.6in. height. Still rising, the gradient now eased to 1 in 189. From here the line curved south to cross the GC (Barnsley Coal Railway) by a similar bridge and then passed beneath Back Lane, up a steady pull at 1 in 140 through the parish of Ryhill to Cow Lane, after which came a descent at 1 in 101 through Cawker Wood set on top of a colliery drift, whereafter the gradient eased to 1 in 144 to milepost No.5. The new line then crossed the H & B by a 26ft span 14ft.6in. high, to reach the Dearne Valley Railway proper at 5m. 6f.2ch. Here the gradient levelled out to 1 in 614.

In due course a halt was provided for Ryhill village, which lay immediately to the west of the line, just south of a convenient overbridge.

With the DVR matters were more complicated as there were several colliery connections to fit in as well as the links at each end. It will be noted

10

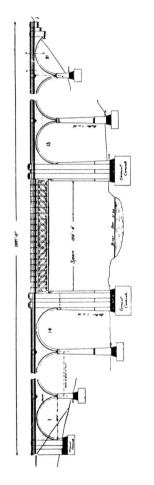

Elevation and Cross Section of Coniabro Viaduct.

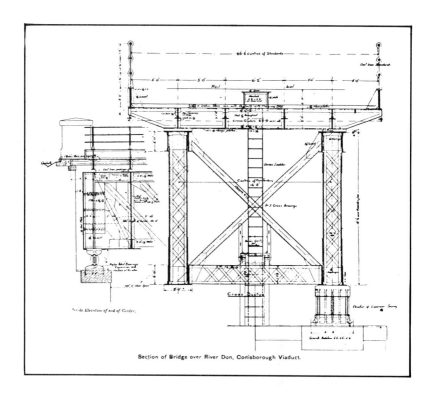

Section of Bridge over River Don, Conisborough Viaduct.

that the DV Jc. was more or less a corridor to the L & Y system, without any intermediate source of revenue apart from Ryhill halt. The DVR was planned originally to link up with the H & BR at Brierley Jc. by means of a flying junction across the up and down main, with Railway No. 1A so-called descending on the north side towards the Hull direction. Railway 1B was to be a reverse curve coming round towards Cudworth, length 2 furlongs 900 chains. In fact, only an orthodox connection was ever put in at Brierley Jc., running off to the east. The line, Railway No.1, ran for two miles mainly falling at 1 in 101 and 1 in 240, then rising at 1 in 200. This first line was 4 miles 4 furlongs in length. Thereafter came Railway No. 2, commencing in the parish of Darfield, mildly undulating and with various short branches off to serve collieries. The S & K was crossed by a 28ft. span 15ft. high. Railway No.3 was described as a short length in the area of Nicholas Lane, Goldthorpe, while No.4 began as 4A among sidings adjacent to the S & K at Hickleton Colliery, to run on for 2 miles 5 furlongs to a point where the Cadeby Colliery branch was to leave as Railway No. 5.

Hereabouts the Dearne was crossed by two bridges with spans of 25ft. and 30ft. as the line ran more or less south east. Railway No.5A ran off to the wharf and lay-bye on the Dearne at Denaby. From Denaby on the main line the formation climbed at 1 in 100 to a viaduct 460yd. long, having a span of 150ft. 100ft. high, from which the line was to fall into a tunnel 760yd. long at gradients of 1 in 166/125 and 150.

The Dearne Valley viaduct at Conisbrough. *C. T. Goode*

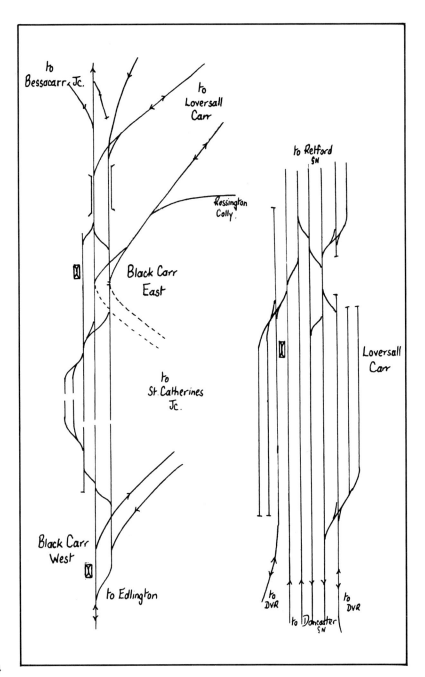

This Railway No.6, of 6 miles 5 furlongs, terminated at Black Carr West Jc. As this last section from Edlington was easily completed it was opened ahead of the heavier works in the Cadeby area and traffic was able to be worked off at the Carr end. Railway No.7 ran across the GN main line to the GN & GE Joint line to Lincoln, while a spur ran down to the aforesaid main line, dividing to arrive on each side of it at Loversall Carr Jc.

The contracting was divided into four, with Naylor Bros. landing the first two sections from Bricrley Jc. to Thurnscoe, 6 miles 17 chains in all. Work began on 1st January, 1899, along to Houghton Main. The section from Denaby to Black Carr was given to H. Lovatt Ltd. and they, of course, had the heavy work to complete. Messrs. Gates & Hogg tendered the sum of £4,919 for the construction of Conisbrough viaduct, which was accepted. The idea of the tunnel was scotched and a deep and impressive cutting appeared instead. In January 1906 the Thurnscoe to Cadeby section opened, with a deep cutting at Harlington and a 2½ mile long embankment 44ft. high along the marshy course of the Dearne, not helped by mining subsidence. Where the Dearne crossed beneath the line the bridge had to be carried on concrete foundations reaching well below ground level.

The Montagus of Melton Hall, over whose land the line ran, insisted on the north side of the embankment being thickly planted with ornamental trees 'to the reasonable satisfaction of the owners'. An ornamental bridge was to be provided over the road at Mexborough Pastures and, more in keeping with the demands of the gentry, a station was to be provided at Barnborough for passengers and goods, suitably connected by telephone and to be open at reasonable hours for the receipt and despatch of telegrams. Any passenger train was to stop for residents and visitors if twenty minutes notice were given from the Hall. Penalty for failure to stop would be £20. Other local requests

Dearne Valley line girder bridge crossing the GN main line at Black Carr Jc.
C. T. Goode

stipulated that floodgates must be provided on the Dearne at the confluence with the Don, while at Butterbusk near Warmsworth on the Conisbrough-Doncaster road, bridge parapets and screens must be six feet high and not used for posters. All other parapets were five feet. Elsewhere things were more laissez-faire, except that the Earl Fitzwilliam had shooting rights over the railway property at Darfield.

A WD loco and brake van come off the Thurnscoe branch towards the main line. G. Warnes

As stated earlier, the Dearne Valley Junction Railway was unspectacular, compared with elsewhere on the new line, and began at Crofton South Jc., a signal box of 64 levers, opened in 1905 and followed by the later Crofton Hall Sidings cabin (48 levers) of 1910. From here the Junction line ran on for 4 miles 1,119yd. to Shafton Jc., a 24 lever cabin set on the east side of the line in the centre of the Y junction with the line from the H & B coming down beside it. The junction line was usually shown as double track, and here were a facing and trailing crossover on each side of the single line connection to the down line. Back at Brierley Jc. the double line came off the H & B in an orthodox manner, but almost immediately ran to Brierley Sidings where there were four or five roads for the exchange of traffic on both sides of the running lines which became one at the south end before reaching Shafton Jc. Just south of Shafton Jc. the line passed under a short tunnel, really an extended bridge beneath the Barnsley-Pontefract road.

The next signal box on the main line which now ran south was that at Hodroyd Colliery, of 36 levers on the west side and with an imposing set of sidings, eight in each direction and all on the east side. After Engine lane had crossed on the skew, Grimethorpe halt was to be found immediately at the bridge on the west side. The layout here appeared in 1913 when doubling of the single line took place. A tramway to the east of the line linked up other colliery sites, one at Brierley village. At 1m. 1,243yd. came Grimethorpe Sidings, one of the original cabins of 1904 with 28 levers.

Just over half a mile beyond came Houghton Sidings with 24 levers, another original cabin of the same year, with a turn-off on the south side facing to Shafton to serve the colliery, and a loop on the opposite side at the Shafton end of the layout.

Old L & Y 0-6-0 No. 52461 on a freight working at Wakefield Kirkgate. Lines to Crofton round to the right.   *C. T. Goode*

Great Houghton halt lay just south of the village and was very conveniently placed. From here the line continued to run due south east towards the rather complicated area of Thurnscoe, Hickleton and Goldthorpe, the first named situated to the north, the centre village somewhat aloof on its hill to the east, topped by its church with three skulls in a glass case under the lych gate and the adjacent Hickleton Hall overlooking what had, after all, become a very grimy and rather squalid valley, while the third was cut through by the DVR from east-west. Here also were two other lines passing north-south and running cheek by jowl with each other. The S & K Joint Line of the Midland and North Eastern on its way between Pontefract and Sheffield managed to pass between Thurnscoe and Thurnscoe East (a rather nasty housing estate) on an overbridge and west of Goldthorpe without building any station in what might well have been a profitable environment. A station on the S & K could well have offered successful trips to Scarborough in the summer, while a great many important towns in the Midlands lay in the opposite direction. There was in fact a rather nice station on the line to the north, at Frickley, a solid affair which served the small village of Clayton and Frickley and Hooton Pagnell Halls. To the south of Goldthorpe lay Bolton-on-Dearne village, which also had a station of its own on the S & K.

The other line which had come upon the scene was the H & B Wath branch from Wrangbrook Jc. which was out looking for coal from the lucrative pits at

17

Frickley, Hickleton and Wath, where there was a terminus for the nebulous passenger traffic. This line came in alongside the S & K, crossing the Thurnscoe-Hickleton road by an overbridge and swinging south west through Goldthorpe beneath the main Darfield road to run on high embankment towards Wath. Between the S & K and H & B sidings were put down for Hickleton Colliery which actually lay to the east of both lines. The H & B rather sensibly sited a station at Thurnscoe which was one of the company's most successful, complete with station signal box, while a little way to the south another cabin kept an eye on the coal sidings. From here seaside excursions were run, usually on to the main line via Moorhouse to Cleethorpes. The LNER, however, closed the section of line south of Thurnscoe, including Wath terminus, between the wars.

So much then for the background of the other railways, not forgetting the roads, through which the new line was to thrust its way. This it did quite well and expensively, coming in from the west at Thurnscoe Jc. (24 levers) where a spur left to run north east to join the S & K at the Hickleton Colliery signal box. This would enable NE running powers to operate to and from collieries west of here. Six hundred yards nearer to Goldthorpe was Nicholas Lane signal box (16 levers) which was probably put in when the passenger service began as it kept company with Goldthorpe Halt on the south side nearby and had two sidings running off at that side for cattle and general merchandise behind the Miners' Welfare and the Halfway Hotel. Before removal the sidings were home to one of the fraternity who seem to be attracted to railway sites, leaving piles of rusty vehicles and similar detritus. For a time the section from Thurnscoe Jc. to Nicholas Lane was single track.

Proceeding east from Goldthorpe halt, the DVR first crossed the S & K before the line passed beneath the main street of the village and the H & B in quick succession. As the H & B had also just emerged from beneath the same main street, there was a near miss for a three level bridge here. From this point the DVR ran almost due east in deep cutting with Hickleton Colliery Sidings (20 levers) in the middle on the south side, a cabin with a fine set of steps up to ground level at the back. The layout here was curiously extended, with the curve in from the colliery sidings guarded by dwarf home and distant signals and a couple of trailing crossovers, everything at hefty pulling distance from the lever frame. A rather similar layout was to be found three quarters of a mile away at Goldthorpe Colliery (32 levers) opened in 1911, where were the same pair of widely spaced crossovers to facilitate the running round of coal trains and a set of five sidings on the north side opposite the cabin. A signal box of similar size was to be found at Barnborough Colliery, which had an impressive array of sidings of its own and a private line which ran off for a good two miles in a south westerly direction to the area of Manvers Main and Wath. The Manvers Main Colliery Company had sunk the shafts at Barnborough in 1911 and gained the first coal in 1914. The private line had opened in 1924 and gained importance as an outlet for Barnborough on closure of the DVR later on. At Barnborough the double track ran past the box for a good distance to beyond Church lane, before the up line fell away into a dead end opposite Harlington halt, named after the small village on the west side. From here the line, now single, ran to the south east and entered the marshy valley of the Dearne, a lazy river with many meanders which caused problems for the engineer. This area was crossed by an embankment 2½ miles long with a maximum height of 44ft., pierced by flood openings and crossing the river twice on its way. The normal level of standing water here

18

A mineral train on the South Yorkshire Joint line crosses the Dearne Valley route at Black Carr, looking east. C. T. Goode

was about five feet, caused by mining subsidence, but could reach 9ft. in times of flood when the Dearne rises rapidly without warning.

Where Pasture road is crossed was the site of Denaby halt at the point where the line again became double, thus there were up and down platforms and the statutary carriage body was on the north side waiting for the incumbent of High Melton Hall to sprint the mile or so down the hill to catch his train. From the Dearne Bridge a path did in fact lead directly uphill to High Melton village for public use, though how often is anyone's guess. The carriage bodies used as shelters at the halts were all similar, in a light cream colour from which the gloss had long since gone, without several panes of glass (if not all), and with evidence of vandalism by the local lads in the shape of missing wood panels and the like. Denaby Siding signal box (28 levers) of 1906 was well placed on the north side to see off the two branches which sprouted from the up line, the first that of about one mile following the Dearne round to its junction with the larger river Don on a rather bleak patch of ground east of Denaby pithead and behind the GC Lowfield Jc. signal box. Here were the wharf and lay-bye to accommodate coal traffic. A short way round the curve from the main line the branch had a blister of double track whereby a train could be run-round if required.

The second branch, to Cadeby colliery ran along parallel to the main line, crossing the Dearne for the third time and giving the appearance of double track for a good distance before fanning out into two or three reception lines, after which it turned away southwards into the colliery yard, crossing the single line of the H & B Denaby branch and an impressive sixteen sidings in the colliery yard by means of a long viaduct before descending into the melee on the south side of it. Cadeby yard must have been one of the busiest in its heyday, and looks well on contemporary plans. The story is not quite ended here, however, as a back run from the DVR Cadeby branch at the point before the aforementioned viaduct began ran north and then north-west up and over the DVR proper to Cadeby Brick Works, crossing the line by a high wooden structure. Looking south, therefore, from the heights of Cadeby Cliff one had immediately below the DVR, then the H & B branch at a slightly lower level, next the Cadeby colliery sidings, the river Don and Conisbrough station on the GC Mexborough-Doncaster line, a most memorable vista backed by rising ground on the other side of the valley.

The ¾ mile long cutting at Cadeby was a challenge to the engineer in that the layers of rock were lubricated by intermediate layers of wet marl which caused resultant instability in the sides of the cutting, so that faults and fissures, as well as the wet clay had to be dug out and settled by means of nine vertical bands of rock filling, each 18ft. deep and 6ft. wide, bound together with cement at intervals along its course.

The illusion of double track ended at a footbridge and the down line carried on alone eastwards, keeping close company with the H & B branch which it crossed by a skew bridge at the mouth of that company's short tunnel, before passing over the GC company's tunnel prior to launching itself over the valley of the Don. The valley vista was further enriched by Conisbrough Castle and by the vastness of Cadeby colliery tip containing many thousands of tons of coal spoil.

Before the GC tunnel is entered from the east, the traveller to Mexborough crosses the Rainbow bridge over the Don and from here had a view of the piece de resistance of the DVR, namely the splendid viaduct of 21 arches, 7 on the east side and 14 on the west, the actual river crossed by a steel lattice girder bridge of 150ft. width. Each arch was 55ft. span, semi circular and of red brick faced with blue, a total of 12 million in all used in construction, along with 3,000 tons of cement. The total length of the viaduct was 1,527ft. and the maximum height above the river was 116 ft., thus obviating the need for an opening span. In order to cover as far as possible against mining subsidence the contractors, Henry Lovatt of Wolverhampton first purchased from the Dalton Main Colliery Company the coal measures over which the viaduct would pass, so that the foundations were on the grey shale and no practical difficulty was encountered in construction here. Good piling was placed at the bases of the piers adjacent to the river to reduce the effect of scouring. Each pier had a taper of 1 in 36 all round to the foundations.

The main work was completed with the assistance of an aerial ropeway, erected by Henderson of Aberdeen, of 1,875ft. stretched between two steel towers of about 80ft. in height at each side of the valley, not unusual in practice, but remarkable as possibly the largest of the kind ever operated in this country. The main cable was 1¾in. in diameter, along with smaller cables for haulage. A special rope, called a button rope conveyed carriage hoops of various sizes which corrected sagging by the main rope when under load, which could be up to three tons if required. A similar method had been used in building the bridge over the Zambesi. The steelwork was provided by John Butler of Stanningley and comprised a bridge of two double N braced girders, with cross girders and rail bearers for the decking. The total steelwork was 311 tons and it was assembled on a timber staging, itself on three piers, one set twelve feet into the bed of the river while the others were on the river banks. Some 40,000 cubic feet of timber were used here and came second hand after doing duty on the construction of the hig level bridge over the Tyne in Newcastle. The timbers then went on to the contractors working on the Leeds Corporation reservoir at Masham.

A scene which is believed to be of the first passenger working at Edlington Halt on the opening day.   *Sheffield City Library*

The steelwork was secured in position on Sunday, 25th February, 1906, and the structure was in use from 17th March, 1909.

The Conisbrough viaduct did quite a lot to enhance the valley across which it passed, and was most impressive complement to the fine hexagonal keep of the castle close by. It was underused for almost all its life and had only a single line of rails to contend with, which swapped sides for some reason before crossing, putting an unusual kink in the smooth running of the trains which did cross it. At the time of writing it still stands, graffiti-ridden and patiently awaiting its fate, probably a messy demolition in due course.

Immediately after leaving the viaduct the line ran on to the side of the valley beneath a footbridge carrying a pleasant pathway along the river and then beneath a high bridge of 61ft.6in. span carrying the Doncaster-Sheffield road to enter a cutting up to 70ft. deep cut out of the solid magnesian limestone rock. A tunnel was suggested here which would have been enormous. Instead, excavation was used and here the same mixture of faults in the rock and wet clays was found as before at Cadeby, and concrete was used to fill in fissures which had been dug out to arrest landslips. The line of the cutting was on a curve of 60 chains radius and memory recalls how hidden things were if one looked across the level field from the road with no sign of the railway below. Most of the excavated material was from the solid rock, and progress was made by drilling holes up to 15ft. depth using compressed air drills. The holes were then filled with gelignite and exploded. The aim was to construct a temporary way of 15ft. width for a few yards, with men widening and emptying spoil into a contractor's railway running in the 'slot'. Alongside this, or further along, another way would be cut and so things developed until the final depth and width were reached. Compressed air for the drills went along a series of pipes up to ¾ mile from the working faces.

When the line was first opened it ran through rather sparsely inhabited and rather beautiful countryside with the small and pretty villages of Loversall, Wadworth and Edlington nearby. The latter was brought rudely into the twentieth century by the opening of Yorkshire Main Colliery 1912 with its headgear and the sprawl of the New Edlington estate. To cater for the new traffic a signal box was erected at Yorkshire Main Siding (32 levers) in 1912 at 3m. 1,450yd. from Denaby, a long rural ride without any signalling. Edlington for Balby halt was well placed by the main road on the single line, with the old coach body and a ground frame on the south side for goods, just within the down distant signal. Later on, from 1916, the immediate area was complicated by the arrival of the H & B and GC Joint line from Aire Jc. to Braithwell Jc. which sported a fair sized goods station at Warmsworth and a full blooded double line curve off to the colliery which crossed both the road and the DVR at Edlington. From the halt the run of line was straight as far as Yorkshire Main Siding, where there was a parallel line off to give access to trains to the colliery, for which there were two outlets facing east and west. The layout was set to the south of the line with the cabin opposite next to a minor road underbridge near Alverley. When the colliery really sprang into action there grew a massive spoil heap which piled up on both sides of this road, fed by an aerial ropeway with a continuous chain of buckets. The affair was memborable, firstly because of the safety net beneath the lines as they crossed the road, to stop hunks of coal from hitting unsuspecting walkers below, and secondly because of the trip lever which would upturn the buckets as they passed it, sending the spoil shooting down to increase the general size.

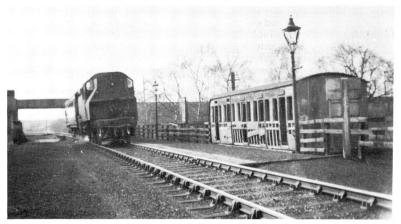

An Ivatt tank engine arrives at Edlington Halt in 1951, Note the advanced state of decay on the waiting shelter.　　　　　　　　　　*C. T. Goode*

From here to the end of the run of the DVR at Black Carr the line ran through undulating country and threaded a pleasant cutting at Loversall with smooth slopes like a lawn, to quote a contemporary commentator when the line was opening. This was the scene of a fatal accident when, on 14th March, 1906 during construction a navvy struck an unexploded charge with his pick, killing three and injuring five others. Otherwise there were no recorded fatalitites during the building of the railway.

At Black Carr West (2m. 326yd.) the DVR reached a complicated set of other lines in this south eastern corner of Doncaster, where the GN East Coast main line to King's Cross sent off the route it owned jointly with the GE to Gainsborough and Lincoln, using a conventional flat junction. Over the top from north to south came the five companies line owned by the GN., GC., Midland, L & Y., and NE., the South Yorkshire Joint Line., a concern which started at Kirk Sandall Jc. on the GC and ran to Shireoaks, again on the GC near Worksop. The DVR ran beneath it from west to east, sending firstly a spur round to the SY Joint southwards to St. Catherine's Jc. from Black Carr West (40 levers) and then running beneath a line from the SY Joint to the down side of the GN proper and also beneath the SY Joint main line to end up at Black Carr East, the largest box on the DVR (60 levers) where a spur from St. Catherine's Jc. ran in, promoted by the GN and L & Y jointly and closed about 1940. The ¾ mile stretch between the two cabins here was enriched by a set of three reception lines on the north side for the interchange of traffic. At one time there was also a small loco. shed here, opened in 1908 when things became operational. At Black Carr West the single line from the west doubled, then went three ways at the signal box, namely right to St. Catherine's Jc., straight ahead to East and left into the yard. Connection between the DVR and the GN was made by a flying junction with a massive girder bridge carrying up and down lines over the GN and to a further flying junction for the GN & GE Joint line at Bessacarr Jc. (35 levers) of 1877. The line ended on the GN at Loversall Carr (68 levers) and down traffic could reach the DVR by a spur up to Black Carr East. This cabin was rebuilt using an LNWR pattern cabin after destruction by fire in 1929.

There was a facing connection to the down spur from Loversall Carr enabling it to be worked either way and giving access to a siding leading to Rossington Colliery, which trailed into the normal direction of running. The signalling here was quite elaborate, much as this attempt to describe a complicated piece of railway topography, and the reader is referred to the accompanying plan which should help matters.

The bridges over the lines at Black Carr are of interest and are impressive structures. That over the GN had a square span of 83ft. 9in. and a skew span of 162ft. 9in. The braced 19ft. deep N main girders had a length of 192ft. and a width of 30ft. 6in. resting on rocker bearings at one end and expansion roller bearings at the other. Clearance beneath was 15ft. The bridge was built up on 1ft. square timber trestles on site and then lifted by 200 ton hydraulic jacks at alternate ends while packing of gradually reducing size was inserted to bring the girders on to the bearings. The total weight of steel here was 479 tons. The DVR bridge over the Lincoln line, carrying a single line this time, was similar to the first but with a skew span of 150ft., a square span of 61ft. 6in. and single N girders. As the single line curved round to join the Joint line at Bessacarr Jc. there was one final touch in the shape of a ground frame and siding off to the Bessacarr Gravel Company's quarry, odd in that the entrance was facing to normal running.

The line was built to first class standards, well appointed with telephones, excellent signal boxes and signalling on which the L & Y prided itself, and with cottages for platelayers and brick shelters for yard staff and lengthmen. Track was 86lb. per yard bullhead laid on good quality ballast gleaned from excavation en route. The total cost for the single line initially was about £700,000. By an Act of 1910 the curve from Black Carr East to the SY Joint now became GN, L & Y and NE, while the other curve from West, opened 7th

An engine and brake stand at Goldthorpe Halt.   *G. Warnes*

October, 1908 was purely L & Y. The principal connections at Black Carr opened 17th May, 1909, later than the main run from Edlington on 19th October, 1908.

During the palmy days between 1912 and 1914 most of the line was doubled, that is between Shafton and Barnborough and a section at Cadeby. These developments coincided with the launching of the passenger service.

WD No. 90421 is seen on a train of empties near Goldthorpe.   *G. Warnes*

The operation of mineral traffic over the DVR can be divided into three areas, namely the shipment of coal out westwards over the L & Y system via Wakefield, eastwards through the junctions at Doncaster, and running powers which enabled other companies' engines to arrive and work off any coal booked via their systems. Particular types of coal might call for block loads from a particular colliery, but it was fairly rare for coal mined at the eastern end of the system to be taken right through to the western end, especially in the early days of working. The working timetable for 1923, at the beginning of the post-Grouping period gave six booked workings of mineral trains, with the empty wagons originating at Crofton Hall Sidings and being taken to Frickley Colliery via Thurnscoe Jc. on to the S & K and also to Grimethorpe Colliery. Three trains were booked to leave Frickley Colliery for Sandhills (Liverpool) via Wakefield at 2.45, 5.00 and 7.03p.m., while two others left Grimethorpe for Sandhills at 4.00 and 6.00p.m. A sixth working was a Class A goods which left Crofton Jc. at 9.10a.m., booked to arrive at Dinnington on the SY Joint line via Black Carr at 10.40a.m., remaining there until returning at 1.30p.m. with a pause at Yorkshire Main at 4.05p.m., getting back to Crofton Jc. at 6.15p.m. Quite a pleasant day out and an enthusiast's delight nowadays.

The running powers of the H & B and of others are not recorded, but the DVR had written down suitable conditions, and general running powers were laid down by the L & Y from Shafton Jc. to Wakefield Kirkgate in an agreement of 1st July, 1901. From such activities the DVR could receive one third of the revenue from through coaching traffic, and 15% from local passenger traffic, and the facilities of Kirkgate station were available. The DVR could run over the H & B from Brierley Jc. to New Monckton and Carlton Collieries near Cudworth, but not to any stations on the H & B or to or from Hull. Here the DVR were to pay 6d. per ton on coal, less one third working expenses, and they were to receive from all other traffic one third revenue on mileage division.

The H & B could run to Houghton and Grimethorpe Collieries via Brierley Jc., but not take traffic bound for Goole or for stations on its own line. Terms were similar to those binding the DVR, but the H & B could allow the DVR a rebate of 2d. per ton in addition to any other agreed payment provided that not less than, 200,000 tons of coal per annum 'shall pass' from the DVR over the H & B line to Hull. This arrangement would be reconsidered if at any time the rate for shipment from Grimethorpe or Houghton Collieries were reduced to 2/5- per ton or less. The L & Y could work to Cudworth Exchange Sidings on the H & B to collect coal from South Hiendley and Hodroyd. If excursions were run over the H & B, then the company would receive 9d. per mile for the engine.

A goods train left Crofton Hall at 6.35a.m. for Cudworth H & B, reversing at Shafton Jc. at 6.55 and again at Brierley Jc. The return working left Cudworth at 8.40a.m. for Crofton Hall, passing Shafton Jc. at 9.20a.m. At the east end there were two interesting pilot trips from Black Carr East Jc. one at 3.30p.m. down to Bessacarr Jc. arrive 3.35, the other at 4.10p.m. arrive Loversall Carr at 4.15. The latter was booked to return at 4.30p.m., though the former seems to have vanished down the Joint line without trace as its return is not recorded! These short workings would indicate a fair amount of activity at Black Carr and would justify the presence of a small engine shed there.

A brace of WDs run with a mineral train at Goldthorpe.   G. Warnes

Reference to the pilot engines sent out during the week on to the DVR will show the amount of traffic which was anticipated:

No. 1.   Off Wakefield shed at 5.45a.m. light engine to Grimethorpe arrive 6.00a.m. Mondays only to work traffic to and from Black Carr as required.

No. 2.   Off Wakefield shed at 6.00a.m. light engine to Crofton Jc., then 6.10a.m. Crofton Jc. to Yorkshire Main with empties, then trips as required.

No. 3.   From Crofton Jc. at 7.00a.m. to work up and down the line as required.

No. 4.   Off Wakefield shed at 6.55a.m. light engine to Crofton Jc., then 7.15a.m. Crofton Jc. to Hodroyd Colliery, then as required.

No. 5.   Off Wakefield shed at 9.30a.m. light engine to Brierley Jc., then as required on DVR.

No. 6.   Off Wakefield shed at 5.45a.m. light engine to Houghton coupled to No. 7. To call at Crofton Hall for brake. Runs Grimethorpe to Crofton Hall arrive 8.00a.m., then at 9.50a.m. to Grimethorpe with brake in front of No. 5, then as required.

No. 7.   Off Wakefield shed at 5.45a.m. MX (6.00a.m. MO) coupled to No. 6 calling at Crofton Hall for brake. Runs with brake to Houghton coupled to No. 6. Runs trip Houghton to Crofton, then with brake to Grimethorpe, then Grimethorpe to Crofton Jc., then 11.00a.m. Crofton Jc. - DV line, then as required.

No. 8.   Off Wakefield shed at 9.05a.m. light engine to Crofton Jc. coupled to No. 45 and Crofton No. 10. Works 9.30a.m. Crofton-Grimethorpe with Barnborough empties, then as required.

No. 9. Off Wakefield shed at 9.05a.m. light engine to Grimethorpe coupled to No. 10. Shunts along DVR and assists at Crofton Hall.

No. 10. Off Wakefield shed at 9.05a.m. light engine to Crofton Hall coupled to Nos. 43 and 45. Leaves at 9.25a.m. with brake for Grimethorpe, then as required.

No. 11. Off Wakefield shed at 11.35a.m. light engine to Crofton Hall, then depart 12.20p.m. with Frickley empties.

No. 12. Off Wakefield shed 12.50p.m. light engine to Crofton Hall, then 1.35p.m. to Grimethorpe with Exchange Sidings empties.

No. 13. Off Wakefield shed at 3.05p.m. SX (1.45p.m.SO) light engine to Crofton Hall, then 3.50p.m. SX (1.45p.m.SO) with Frickley empties.

The shed staff at Wakefield would have a lively time in ensuring the prompt departure of all the above, the activity of which showed the importance of the new line and its vital links with the new collieries, nearly all of which were in competition with other companies such as the Midland and GC who had their own branches serving the yards. The NER had a foothold in the Goldthorpe area by way of the S & K through Pontefract, and had running powers to Houghton Main. The GN would work supplies of loco. coal from Black Carr round to the big engine shed at Doncaster, these from Yorkshire Main, though the GC., not to be outflanked, ran coal similarly from Yorkshire Main over their joint line with the H & B, taking a zig-zag course firstly to Sprotborough Jc., then propelling to Hexthorpe Jc. up the avoiding line and finally running right way into Doncaster Carr.

Local working out of Doncaster at Yorkshire Main Siding Box.   *C. T. Goode*

Large nameboard in evidence at Denaby Halt.   *H. C. Casserley*

The GC branch to Houghton Main Colliery was quite a long one, running from Stairfoot Jc. on the Barnsley-Mexborough line and striking out across country for 2 or 3 miles to the north east and crossing the MR main line in the process. Access to the coal yard here could be potentially dangerous, as witness the extract from the Working Appendix:-

'Grimethorpe Rifle Range: Whenever this range is in use, the Military Authorities will exhibit a large red flag on the footbridge which crosses the branch. Drivers of trains working over the branch must keep a careful lookout and, if approaching the danger zone, they observe the red flag is exhibited, must whistle loudly, whereupon firing will cease.' One hopes the latter assurance was always implemented!

While consulting the Working Appendices, other gems were found which concerned the DVR arrangements more closely:

'At the Bessacarr Gravel Siding trains calling for traffic purposes must call the attention of the Gravel Company's staff by giving one whistle when approaching the siding.' On the nearby Rossington Colliery branch which was worked by one engine in steam there was a crossbar signal worked by the colliery staff. Along with this was a token for use, fixed between the GN down main line and the Loversall Carr line some 20yd. in the rear of the Black Carr East Inner Home signal.

Trains from Tickhill (SY Joint) to Rossington Colliery of up to 40 wagons could run directly from St. Catherine's Jc. to Black Carr West, and then be propelled to Rossington Colliery over the up main and the single line, which would explain the facing point for two way working at Black Carr East and Rossington Colliery, where presumably the train could be run round for shunting. Drivers of such trains could whistle at Tickhill station to advise how they should be handled at Black Carr.

From 7th October, 1908 the L & Y could work on and off the SY Joint line and were, from 11th November, 1908, able to move local traffic between Dinnington and Maltby Collieries.

At Cudworth North Jc. on the H & B drivers of trains bound for the DVR via Brierley Jc. had to whistle one crow, while those bound for the DVR from the east had to give two short blasts and one crow at Hemsworth. The tunnel beneath the main road on the DVR at Shafton was long enough to have a gong inside it to enable loco. movements to be controlled remotely from Shafton Jc. with one beat for stop, two beats for 'set back' and three for 'draw ahead'. Staffs which were carried by drivers on the single line runs were all square section and used from Hickleton Colliery Sidings box to the yard, Shafton to Brierley Jc. and on the two branches from Denaby Siding. Tablets were in use for the lines serving New Hodroyd Colliery, Goldthorpe Colliery, Barnborough Tip, Harlington Ground Frame and Edlington Colliery.

As mentioned earlier, a great deal of coal traffic went over the Pennines to Liverpool and there were plain and strict rules as to how loads were to be handled. To begin with, loads were brought either to Crofton Hall or the Calder Bridge Loop where they were made up into 850 ton trains running as far as Hebden Bridge, where they were again reduced to 745 ton loads which then went en bloc through to Sandhills. With two Class A engines in charge, the load could be increased to 940 tons throughout. Much of the coal was destined for home use, keeping, say, a couple of Cunard liners steaming on up to half a million tons a year, or a small tramp steamer in 8,000 tons per annum. Thus, much of the annual estimated output of 280 million tons of coal would go to Liverpool, Grimsby, Hull or Goole to keep the stokeholds supplied with fuel. Other times, other customs indeed.

The passenger service seems just to have developed naturally on this, essentially a mineral railway, and halts at rail level, consisting of a layer of

Hughes railmotor, No. 10600.   *Collection – C. T. Goode*

Interior of Yorkshire Main Siding Box.   *C. T. Goode*

ashes, lamps, a nameboard, fencing and an old coach body made up the stopping place. The bodies were in a pale yellow colour, and looked decidedly knocked about after the last war, with little spent on their upkeep. The nameboards were big and splendid, especially at Denaby and Edlington (both Illustrated). Possibly local representation had gone out for such a service, and both the L & Y and DVR had hastened to fill the requirement, pressing into service one of the Hughes rail motors fitted with retractable steps work by the engine's vacuum system. The L & Y were a dab hand at running these little units on their branches, and up to 18 were built of these engine-cum-coach affairs. The steam unit had 3ft. 7½in. wheels on an eight foot wheelbase driven by two cylinders 12" X 16". Water carried was 550 gallons, along with 15 cwt. of coal. One of the chief performers on the DVR was L & Y No. 13, later No. 10610 which was built in March 1907 and rebuilt in 1912.

Trespassers' Notice at Goldthorpe.   *C. T. Goode*

Halts appeared at Ryhill (6 miles), Grimethorpe (8½ miles), Great Houghton (11¾ miles), Goldthorpe & Thurnscoe (13½ miles), Harlington (15¾ miles) and Edlington (20¼ miles), with Denaby following later on. All were more or less convenient for the villages they served, except Denaby which, one suspects, was created to placate Melton Hall. Goldthorpe enjoyed a prime site in the village, but had closed by 1949 and had been closed on the Ordnance Survey map two years earlier!

The local press had noted the opening of the new service and stated:

'This service promises to be of the greatest value to colliery workers as it runs through the heart of a coalpit district. A dozen or more important

31

Typically L & Y – Yorkshire Main Siding Box.   *C. T. Goode*

collieries will, by means of this passenger service, be rendered far more accessible than before.'

'A great deal of interest was taken in the initial run of the Dearne Valley motor train which is being used to connect Wakefield with South Yorkshire. The service opened on Monday (3rd June, 1912), the first train leaving Wakefield Kirkgate at 8.15a.m., and a goodly number of passengers were taken to the 'halts' en route for Edlington (for Balby).'

'The train is a single, saloon-like coach comfortably fitted, with cane rattan seats and it is drawn by a small engine, while an observation compartment at the other end of the coach obviates the necessity of changing the engine at the journey's end. The journey to Edlington takes 55 min. and it links up with the City of Wakefield villages with which rail communication has hitherto been almost impossible.' The report went on to describe the twenty or so passengers, quite a motley crew if it to be believed; a clergyman, ladies and two policemen with four handcuffed prisoners. Later in the day there was quite a rush of passengers between Goldthorpe and Wakefield.'

The original service was four return runs out from Wakefield and back again, and the 1914 service, which took 56 min. was as follows:

| Wakefield dep: | 8.10a.m. | 10.25 | 1.15p.m. | 3.20p.m. | 9.30 SO. |
| Edlington dep: | 9.13 | 11.28 | 2.15 | 4.20 | 10.30 SO. |

By 1923 the service had remained roughly the same, minus the 3.20p.m. and 4.20p.m. return trip, but two years later under LMS control things were at their best ever as follows:

Wakefield dep:	8.10a.m.	10.25	1.05p.m.	3.28	6.05	9.30 SO	9.45 SO.*
Edlington dep:	9.13	11.28	2.12	4.25	8.15	10.30*SO	10.36 SO

* was a short working out to Goldthorpe and back, giving the area's Saturday night drinkers a good chance to get home safely. Unless Wakefield shed had two Hughes rail motors, then this service would be worked by a 2-4-2T and coach.

Two further years are given below for comparison; thereafter the service remained more or less similar until closure in September, 1951.

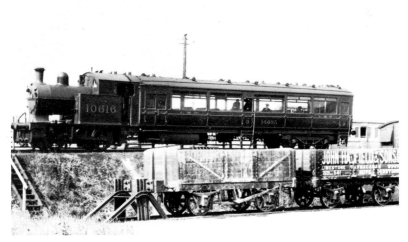

Hughes Railmotor at Edlington Halt. 29/6/33   *H. C. Casserley*

Spring 1935.

Wakefield dep:	8.10a.m.	10.25	1.05p.m.	3.30	6.05	9.45 SO*
Edlington dep:	9.13	11.28	2.13	4.37	8.15	10.30 SO*

Winter 1937

Wakefield dep:	8.10a.m.	10.25	1.05p.m.	3.50*	5.45	8.15*	10.06SO*
Edlington dep:	9.13	11.28	2.13	4.40*	6.50	9.05*	10.57SO*

* to or from Goldthorpe. A wait of between three and eight minutes was booked for return runs at Denaby.

The last service into Wakefield was permitted to stop at Crofton South Jc. when required to pick up loco. men from the sheds.

In February 1914 a public enquiry was held at Barnsley County Court into an application by the Promoters of the Dearne Valley Light Railway, a company concerned with street traction, to operate a street tramway linking the villages of Wath, Bolton-on-Dearne and Goldthorpe, a venture which had nothing to do with the railway under review, but which enjoyed some success. Railway interests were represented by Mr. A de C. Parmiter for the DVR and Mr. M. H. S. Moss-Blundell for the H & BR, both of which companies had passenger services running in the area in question. A local practitioner, Dr. William Craik was called and examined by Mr. Jeeves for the Promoters of the Order. A section of what followed is recorded here to give some idea of public feeling at the time in regard to what the DVR had to offer:

Have you not got a halt at Goldthorpe?
- That is not on a main line at all.
That takes you to Wakefield?
- It takes you to Wakefield, but it does not bring you back. You are landed in Wakefield for the night.
I thought Goldthorpe itself was rather a good shopping and amusement centre?
- It is very good for shopping, and recently a little amusement has been introduced.
A revival has set in recently?
- Yes.
I understand they have a Hippodrome there?
- Yes.
And a Picture Palace as well?
- Yes, and they want it.
They are gluttons for amusement in Goldthorpe?
- A man, when he has been down a pit for five days, wants some amusement.
So a revival has set in there?
- Yes.

(Moss-Blundell now questions:)
Now, how many trains a day do you say there are to Wakefield?
- I don't know, but I am right about there not being a train back.
You can leave Wakefield at 3.30p.m. and get to Goldthorpe at 3.55?
- Yes, but Insurance Committee meetings are never over before 5.30 or 6.00, and it is 8.30 before I can get a train and then I am not home till nine.
And if there was a demand for people to go there, there would be more trains?
- Possibly.
Goldthorpe is a large village?
- I should call it a town.
And as we know, rail facilities cannot grow very rapidly?
- I do not think they have grown with the place at all.

Both DVR and the L & YR were at pains to point out that there were no proper stations on the line as it was not adapted for the running of passenger trains. However, an attempt was being made to offer some travel facilities to local inhabitants. A fare table of single fares was produced:

	Ryhill	Grimethorpe	Gt. Houghton	Goldthorpe & Th.	Harlington	Edlington
Wakefield	6d.	8½d.	1/-.	1/1½d.	1/3½d.	1/8d.
	Ryhill	2½d.	Cd.	7½d.	9½d.	1/2d.
		Grimethorpe	3½d.	5d.	7d.	11½d.
			Gt. Houghton	1½d.	3½.d	8d.
				Goldthorpe & Th.	2d.	6½d.
					Harlington	4½d.

In the magazine 'Trains Illustrated' of August 1951 Mr. Geoffrey Oates wrote an article on the DVR and its passenger service, and a portion of it is reproduced here, with due acknowledgements to the author:

One Saturday shortly before closure I went down to Edlington to sample the service. On arrival from Wakefield, the push-and-pull ran through the station to the signal box beyond to exchange tablets, as the line is only single track. For my journey a push-and-pull fitted Ivatt 2-6-2 tank, No. 41283 was the motive power for an ancient L & Y saloon. As the train drew to a standstill at the halt and I prepared to clamber up to the coach from the low platform, some steps folded beneath the door suddenly opened out. Once aboard the carriage I discovered that the steps, of which there is a set for each of the four doors, were worked by vacuum, with a separate control handle for each door. My sole companions at the start of the trip turned out to be a railfan from Wakefield and the guard-cum-conductor, who collected fares and issued tickets to all passengers picked up en route.

A heavy coal train westbound at Harlington. G. Warnes

The push-and-pull was no flyer, for it was allowed 62 minutes for the 20¼ miles, including stops, and unfortunately a goods train travelling ahead of us made the second half of the run more lethargic still. Twenty minutes were lost waiting for signals, but despite this setback we arrived at Wakefield only 16 minutes late. We set off promptly from Edlington and were soon traversing a high and impressive viaduct over the Don at Conisbrough, with an excellent view of the castle, which was chosen by Sir Walter Scott for one of the principal scenes of 'Ivanhoe'. Before Denaby Halt, closed for passengers since 1949, the train ran under the Sprotborough-Shireoaks (sic) and Doncaster-Sheffield lines, then bridged the Hull-Aire Jc.-Mexborough route. It was now in the Dearne Valley proper, and the track hugged the bank of the small river for about two miles. After Harlington Halt, which we passed without stopping, the line became double track, and proceeded beneath the old Swinton & Knottingley Joint line of the LMS & LNER, to which it is linked by a spur. Just before this junction stands Goldthorpe & Thurnscoe Halt, which we reached with seven minutes to spare, so that the conductor was able to shout an encouraging 'Plenty of time!' to a lady running for the train.

Our load increased by two passengers, we were again two minutes ahead of time at the next halt, Great Houghton, which was bare of passengers. About two miles further on, at Grimethorpe Colliery Sidings, adverse signals stopped the train for four minutes, which the engine used to advantage by taking water. Eventually we passed the empty Grimethorpe Halt at low speed, two minutes late, but after threading a very short tunnel we were halted once more at Shafton Jc., and it was two minutes before the signal cleared. It was here that the former Hull & Barnsley line, which bridges our line, made physical connection with the Dearne Valley Railway, over which it enjoyed running powers.

We arrived at Ryhill, the last halt of the route, three minutes late, and were joined by five adults and two children. Adverse signals kept us waiting for 12 minutes, and there was a further two minutes delay at Wintersett, about half a mile further on. Crossing the ER Doncaster-Leeds main line, we reached Crofton Jc. where the Dearne Valley section terminated and were able at last to pass the offending goods train which was in the sidings. Our route made a triangular junction with the ex L & Y route from Goole, and there is a spur to the ex LMS Sheffield-Leeds line above at this point. At Wakefield sheds (26a) we came to another halt, this time to pick up four railwaymen, and then drew up in Kirkgate station at 3.31 p.m.

The area we had covered, not particularly picturesque, consisted mainly of colliery districts and there were many short branches en route serving the nearby pits. The line, graded quite steeply, deals with a moderate volume of freight traffic, and owing to the danger of colliery subsidence, speeds rarely exceed 40 mph., but obviously the passenger service could have been accelerated. It is not surprising, therefore, to find the service withdrawn, particularly as the trains were so infrequent and the fares so high; the so-called 'cheap day return' from Edlington to Wakefield cost 5s.6d., while the single fare was 4s.3d., yet the ER charged no more than 2s.6d. for a 'cheap day return' from Doncaster to Wakefield Westgate, a journey of speed, comfort and convenience far above the DVR push-and-pull standards.'

Black Carr West cabin, looking west.

T. T. Sutcliffe

Getting away over the S & K bridge.
                                                                G. Warnes

WD. 2-8-0 No. 90617 on westbound mineral working approaching Conisbrough Viaduct.
                                                                G. Warnes

In later correspondence to the magazine Mr. Oates corrects his wrong labelling of the lines crossed by the DVR in the Doncaster area, and indicates that the line was originally due to lose its passenger service in June 1951, prior to the actual date of 10th September, Mr. A. T. Booth also wrote in, with the following:

'Until the Ivatt Class 2 tank engines Nos. 41283/4 arrived at Wakefield last year, ex L & Y 2-4-2 tanks Nos. 50650/6 were used on the Dearne Valley line.

May I point out that the cheap day return fare is 4s.3d. and not 5s.6d.? It is irrelevant to compare the ER Wakefield-Doncaster service with the Dearne Valley line, as the latter is not intended to serve Doncaster. Edlington Halt provides a useful link between the nearby Miners' Welfare centre and the mining villages along the line. The fact that the Centre's cricket team were playing away on the occasion of Mr. Oates' visit accounted for the absence of passengers south of Goldthorpe. With the exception of Ryhill there is no competing bus service between Wakefield and the Dearne Valley villages; the road journey involves changing in Barnsley.'

Mr. Oates had the last word on the subject. He said that public transport had made it possible for people in Edlington to go by bus to Doncaster and then go by rail to Wakefield Westgate at a total of 3s.2d., 1s.1d. less than by the Dearne Valley push-and-pull. It was not altogether irrelevant to compare 4s.3d. for 20¼ miles and 2s.6d. for 19¼ miles when the question of convenience, comfort and service were considered - surely the DVR fares should have been as low, if not lower, that the ER cheap day rate? Although there were no direct bus routes linking the Dearne Valley mining districts with Wakefield, it must not be overlooked that it was the bus routes to Doncaster or Barnsley which had made it cheaper for those residents to shop at these towns rather than go by train to Wakefield.

While one could see the sense in siting the halts where they ultimately happened to be, the reasons for placing the one at Edlington were somewhat obscure. Miners for Yorkshire Main Colliery would be available locally and few would come to work there from any of the other points on the line. For a time chars-a banc left Cleveland Street in Doncaster to convey miners to Edlington at 1s. per week, and it is obvious from the layout of lines at Black Carr that there was no intention to run any train service to or from Doncaster, thus eliminating those who might wish to use the L & Y trains for shopping or social purposes in the town. Possibly, then, at a period when little was thought of a three mile walk, Edlington Halt was placed where it was as the most convenient spot for Doncaster and in fact only one mile from the Warmsworth tram terminus.

In spite of everything, however, the DVR 'Titanic' had its adherents and on 8th August, 1946 a small squad of members of the Doncaster Grammar School Railway Society had a run on the branch, from Edlington to Wakefield and back, the author being fortunate enough to discover a note on the event which listed the party as Messrs. Speer, Brown B. K., Newham, Francis, Howlett, Morris, Walton, Broadhead, Robinson, Blakey, Scholey and self. As mentioned above the passenger service ceased on 10th September, 1951, given the last rites by a further group of enthusiasts who were unlisted on this occasion. Thereafter the line soldiered on, moving many tons of coal, some of it through from Rossington to Wakefield and most of it in the hands of the WD Class 2-8-0 locomotives which did sterling service with little maintenance

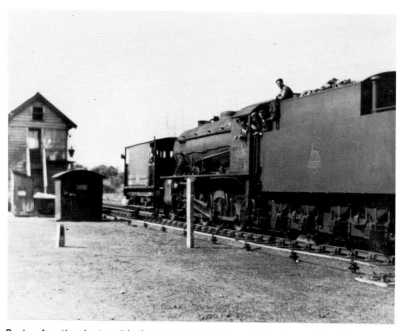

Party of enthusiasts with the pick-up working at Barnborough.   G. Warnes

Conisbrough Viaduct.   *Heyday Publishing Company*

both here and on the H & B section, gradually losing their cabside numbers beneath layers of grime and rust.

Eventually 'Rationalisation' set in, and it was decided to route the coal differently. A new double line junction was installed near to Houghton Main Colliery on the Midland main line where, from Dearne Valley North Jc. a line struck off towards the DVR, then split into each direction at Dearne Valley South Jc., north to Grimethorpe Colliery and south to Goldthorpe. Thus the old through run could be closed from 11th July, 1966 and traffic taken off via the MR route. The spur from Thurnscoe to Hickleton had closed two years earlier after a fire at Thurnscoe Jc. The section of line from Yorkshire Main to Black Carr West remained open for the colliery traffic which ran round to St. Catherine's after the closure of the spurs to the main lines at Black Carr in May 1972. A change of plan enabled Goldthorpe coal to reach the S & K by way of a relayed section of line towards Hickleton Colliery sidings, enabling the Dearne Valley South-Goldthorpe section to be closed on 14th May, 1978. Rails were also put down again on the DVR viaduct over the GN main line as a flying junction, off the Joint line from Lincoln. A line was also put down from St. Catherine's to the down side of the GN at about the same time, in May 1977 and the whole area, some of it with bi-directional sections, was controlled from the Doncaster power box.

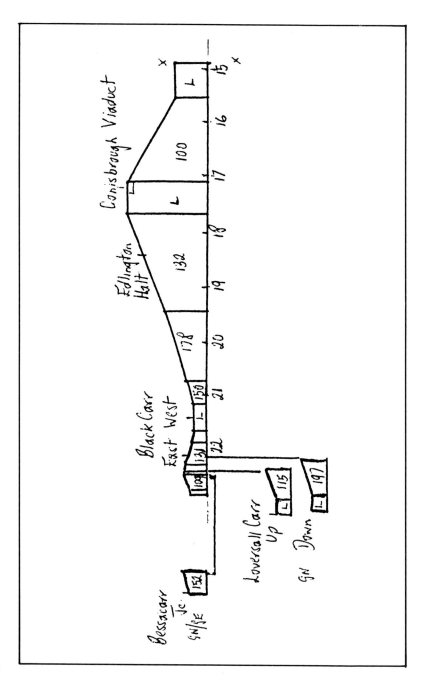

Conisbrough Viaduct

Edlington Halt

Black Carr
East West

Bessacarr
Jc.
GN/GE

Loversall Carr
Up
GN   Down

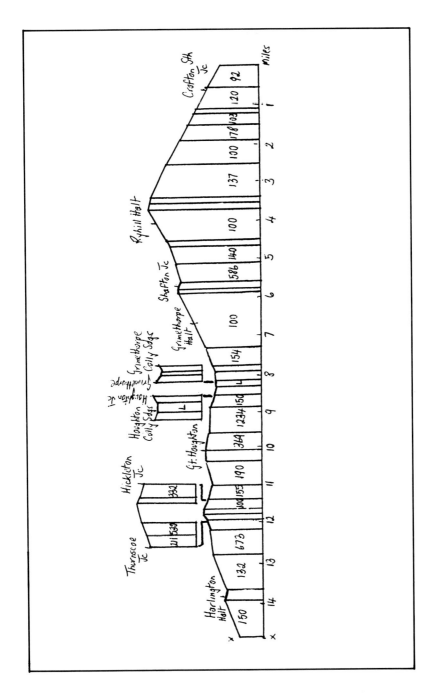

THE RAILWAY EXECUTIVE - EASTERN REGION

My Ref. D4/Winter
1951/E/LM.

District Passenger Superintendent,
Victoria Station,
Sheffield.4.

22nd August, 1951.

Passenger Train Arrangements - Winter 1951/52
(L.M. Operating Area).

Will you please note that commencing with the Winter
1951/52 Time Tables, September 10th, Dearne Valley Line
will be closed for passenger train traffic, and the following
trains will be withdrawn :-

```
 8.10am        Motor Wakefield (K) to Edlington
10.25am        Motor Wakefield (K) to Edlington
 1.5pm         Motor Wakefield (K) to Edlington
 3.50pm        Motor Wakefield (K) to Goldthorpe
 5.45pm(SO)Motor Wakefield (K) to Edlington
 5.45pm(SX)Motor Wakefield (K) to Goldthorpe
 8.30pm(SO)Motor Wakefield (K) to Goldthorpe

 9.18am(EX)Motor Edlington to Wakefield  (K)
 9.27am(FO)Motor Edlington to Wakefield  (K)
11.33am(SO)Motor Edlington to Wakefield  (K)
 2.13pm       Motor Edlington to Wakefield  (K)
 4.40pm       Motor Goldthorpe to Wakefield (K)
 6.50pm(SO)Motor Edlington to Wakefield  (K)
 7.17pm(SX)Motor Goldthorpe to Wakefield (K)
 9.20pm(SO)Motor Goldthorpe to Wakefield (K)
```

K. A. KINDON.

Designed and Printed by Swannack, Brown & Co. Ltd., 13a Anlaby Road, Hull. HU1 2PJ